Social Isolation

How to deal with it and be Highly Productive

EDIN BROW R

TABLE OF CONTENTS

Dedication

First and foremost I thank the Almighty for the prospects, knowledge and guidance to write this book. I am forever indebted to my wife who has never been tired of pushing me to progress. I owe my gratitude to my beloved sister who passed away during the process of completing this book. This book would not be resumed without constant support from friends and colleagues who motivated me to complete the book for the benefit of those who are desperately in need of a push to pursue their passion. I am also thankful to all those who helped me to publish this book successfully. It will never be complete without thanking the readers who need guidance to conquer their dreams and turn every single day into a productive day.

Author's Note

This is a book about how to deal with social isolation and be highly productive. The author focuses on how to plan wisely and pursue the passions and dreams in your life during isolation. During this period of isolation, you may have questions to ask yourself such as:

Am I feeling bored?

Am I feeling stressed?

How can I be productive during this stage of my life?

Do I procrastinate doing things?

How am I going to pursue my passions and goals to fulfill my dreams?

How can I make my life more meaningful?

There may be even many other questions which linger in your mind right at this time. You have to ponder on the things which hinder your progress and set aside your anxieties and worries that pull you down. The best thing that can be done is to give time to self-realization and contemplate on works which make you feel satisfied and comfortable.

The chapters in this book will be of much importance to Craft Your Days, Chase the Lazy Goose, Clock Your Time, Beat the Stress, and Drive your Emotions to the destined path of glory and success. If you want to be highly productive then you have to change the style of working towards your desired goals.

Think about the ways in which you can fulfill your hopes and dreams. There are various steps to be followed in order to be highly productive. Some of the ways are by reinforcing our regular habits, planning, analyzing, self-realizing, exercising, refreshing and rejuvenating.

The author shares his experiences and ideas to deal with isolation and be highly productive at any stage of your life. There is no definite road map to success but there are a lot of ways to overcome hurdles and reach the horizon of success.

Foreword

Social Isolation: How to deal with it and be highly productive is a book that kindles the fire to pursue the passions and dreams of your life which have been put to halt for a long time. This book helps you to identify and overcome the barriers around you through strong motivation and guidance. The main focus of the author is on how to deal with your thoughts and emotions like stress, anxiety, boredom and other personal issues that hinders the progress of personal and professional life.

This book contains chapters on how to craft your days, chase the lazy goose, clock your time, beat stress, and steer your emotions in the direction of success and glory. You will find the path to success if you invest your time, ideas, and actions in analyzing and rescheduling your activities.

As mentioned earlier, there are various ways that transform us to be productive such as reinforcing our regular habits, planning, analyzing, self-realizing, exercising, refreshing and rejuvenating. Definitely, this book ends with a high thinking, "We may be born as an ordinary person but we are made as an extraordinary person through our actions and deeds."

Testimonials

In a time when technology dominates our lives, we often find ourselves more connected digitally but increasingly disconnected socially. This book serves as a beacon of hope, guiding readers through the intricate web of social isolation and offering practical strategies to break free from its grip. The author's deep understanding of the subject is evident throughout the book. They expertly navigate the complexities of social isolation, exploring its causes and consequences with empathy and insight. By weaving together compelling stories, relevant research, and thought-provoking analysis, the author sheds light on the profound impact of social isolation on our mental, emotional, and physical well-being.

What sets this book apart is its unwavering focus on solutions. It goes beyond merely highlighting the problems of social isolation and provides a comprehensive roadmap for reconnecting with others and nurturing genuine connections. From practical tips to cultivate meaningful relationships to exploring the role of technology in fostering or hindering social bonds, the author equips readers with invaluable tools to overcome isolation and build a rich and fulfilling social life. I found the book to be both informative and inspiring. It not only deepened my understanding of social isolation but also motivated me to take action in my own life. The author's compassionate voice and gentle encouragement make it feel like you have a supportive friend guiding you every step of the way.

- Hemamalini I
English & Soft skills Trainer, India

This is a unique and highly useful guidebook that provides valuable practical advice for both the aspiring and working people. While it's true that 'writing is easy but thinking is hard,' Edin brow has made the 'thinking' part that much easier. This book help me finally understand the term Social Isolation. His book made it so clear and easy to understand. I was very pleasantly surprised by the level of detail about Social Isolation.

- Ramesh S
Financial Consultant

"Social Isolation" is a must-read for anyone seeking to understand the profound impact of isolation in our society and seeking practical strategies to combat it. Whether you're struggling with loneliness yourself or want to support others in breaking free from social isolation, this book offers profound insights and actionable advice that will undoubtedly make a positive difference in your life and the lives of those around you."

- Stefan C
General Manager

INTRODUCTION

Social Isolation is a state of physical and particularly mental alienation from society and people. It is different from loneliness which is a mental and emotional disconnection. You can have a feeling of isolation even when people are around you and such a kind of isolation is termed as Emotional Isolation. These two forms of isolation have startling similarities but also significant distinctions. In fact, social isolation may occur due to loss of a family member, life partner, friend, or someone dear through death or it may even happen because of confinement. It can also happen at old age when isolated from dear ones and society.

During the period of isolation, you may feel that it is hard to manage but you can overcome it through your strong will power which has to be tapped at the right moment. There are times when you feel lonely and emotionally down. You may be physically or emotionally far from human interactions. If you are physically away from people and society, you can connect to them through modern technology. But, if you are emotionally detached then you need to connect to the right kind of people. You need to have a constant connection with family, friends, relatives and others in order to keep yourselves away from the feeling of loneliness. However, as days pass on, you need to redesign your positive connections.

This book is envisioned to deal with social isolation and to be highly productive. Through the chapters, we can understand how to plan wisely and pursue your passions and dreams in your life during isolation. Before starting to read the chapters, you have to think of your current life and ponder the following questions:

Am I feeling stressed?

Am I feeling bored?

Do I procrastinate doing things?

How can I be productive at this stage of my life?

How am I going to pursue my passions and goals to fulfill my dreams?

Being highly productive doesn't happen all of a sudden. You need to take the first step through breaking the walls that hinder your progress. The chapters in this book will throw light on planning, implementations, changing habits, overcoming laziness, procrastination, boredom, stress, and anxiety. It also gives you tips to manage your time, emotions, health, and personal well-being.

I assure you that this book will prepare you thoroughly to conquer your dreams in a confident way. Together we can pursue our dreams by overthrowing the hurdles in our life and be productive through self-realization, planning, analyzing, exercising, refreshing and rejuvenating.

"Ordinary people think merely of spending time, great people think of using it."

- Arthur Schopenhauer

CHAPTER 1

CRAFT YOUR DAY

Productivity is highly possible when you craft for your day wisely. Crafting your day lies on the principle of planning systematically and meticulously depending on your passions and dreams. The primary step to craft your day according to your aspirations is to wake up early. It is considered as an easy task for few people but for most of the people getting up early is a herculean task. Starting your day early gives you the strength, energy and mind to be productive. Highly productive people make the best use of their morning routine to achieve success.

"If you want to make your dreams come true, the first thing you have to do is wake up." - J.M. Power

I had a strong desire to achieve something worthy in life before I die. I couldn't figure out the exact thing until I was financially and personally broke down into pieces. It happened multiple times and it has been a never ending process. But I realized that every time when I feel low there is that one thing which pulls me out of the miry clay and makes me press forward. That was the moment when I really started to love my beloved Dr. APJ Abdul Kalam quote, "Dream is not that which you see while sleeping, it is something that does not let you sleep."

During the period of Isolation, we all tend to ignore the best part of our life. We always tend to think about the lost things rather than appreciate and uphold the things which are within our reach. In fact, we waste a great amount of time during isolation through unproductive activities. We could save and manage those times to be highly productive. If you are not able to manage your day properly then you may be a victim of stress, pressure, anxiety and fear. My boss used to say that only a lazy guy says he is busy. A busy person finds time in his schedule and he relaxes even while doing work. You will be able to handle any kind of pressure if you know how to deal with time.

Crafting your day

Time once lost is lost forever. You cannot redeem time with anything in the world. Time flies away, turning everything old. Your thoughts and emotions turn into a dunghill if you are not able to conquer your dreams. If you are able to manage your time wisely, the road to success is not far ahead. Every pain you undergo turns into joy when you look back at the path you have

6

traveled. Never forget the lessons learnt during this journey because it is the strongest basement. Remember, nothing can stand before the test of time. Many people work hard to master time, yet it is not readily mastered but can be managed with caution. Follow the following steps to be highly productive in your personal and professional life. Make it a habit by following it regularly.

Step 1

Spending time judiciously is a key strategy in Planning and decision making. It is a wise idea to create a "to do" list and "not to do" list.

Step 2

Before the start of the day, sit down for 5 to 10 minutes with a piece of paper and create a "to do" list. Decide the things which you can accomplish realistically. Think about the goals which will make you feel that you have been productive and successful at the end of the day. Note down those points to proceed further.

Step 3

Next, check out your calendar and schedule the things into your time slots. Prioritize and Reprioritize your list based on your daily schedule.

Step 4

Set a reminder or alarm to go off every hour or two. Take short breaks to rest and ask yourself whether you have been productive for the last one or two hours. Look at your list and resume your next tasks.

Step 5

Take time to review the tasks accomplished by the end of the day. Reviewing your day will help you to be more productive day by day.

Be focused and follow every step to make your day productive. If you are able to add up a few more steps that decorate your day, you are nowhere but on the path to the success of your dreams.

"Focused, productive successful mornings generate focused, productive, successful days – which inevitably create a successful life." - Hal Elrod, The Miracle Morning

Prioritize

You need to prioritize the tasks based on significance and seriousness. Do the demanding and urgent work first followed by other tasks; by doing so you will be able to keep your stress level down.

When you plan for the day, keep in mind these important aspects such as family & friends, health, meditation and usage of electronic gadgets especially your mobile phone. In today's world, usage of mobile phones has shattered most of the dreams. It is the real time-spoiler as well as life-spoiler. Set screen time and minimize the usage.

Take all your workable ideas and structure them into action plans. Organize and evaluate your ideas in order to be productive.

Focus

Focusing on one work at a time is the best practice. Try to avoid distractions such as noises, games, unwanted thoughts.

Separate your daily schedule with the Main list.

Never forget that "You master the day; the day doesn't master you."

You are not going to achieve everything in one day. Just be cool, master the single day and keep practicing it every day.

Sometimes you may lack focus, just relax and clear the fog. Try listening to melodious music and carry on any creative work of art to soothe your heart and mind. Have a cup of coffee/tea to boost your energy. Reduce your mental fatigue while working on your tasks.

"The secret of your
future is hidden in your
daily routine."

- Mike Murdock

Managing Time

You need to structure and manage your time effectively in order to be productive. Perform the right task at the right time.

Pen down exactly how much time you have planned to spend on each task, then total it up to get the exact number of hours.

Get your most important task done at the start of the day, then the rest of the day turns out to be more fruitful.

When you make the best use of time then it turns out to be a productive day.

Setting Deadlines

Deadlines force you to work harder and more effectively as the deadline approaches.

A goal or project without a deadline is considered as a work of futility. Keeping a deadline is not compulsory because some may think of it as pressure. It is for those who procrastinate and put aside their works till the last minute. Make promises to other people that you will do the task by the deadline. When you do so, you are trying to motivate yourself to complete the task.

Reflect and Review

Reflect and review your progress to be effective, by doing so you will be able to keep track of your plans.

Decide to do something productive for the day and get it done. It is better. It's ok even if you do something less productive. You need to feel proud that you have done something at the end of the day.

Crafting your day is like laying a strong foundation for an enduring building. It can withstand calamities or stand tall amidst adversities. Planning deliberately in accordance with your interests and goals is what it means to "craft" your day.

There will not be any change until you decide to act on your dreams and wishes. Your progress depends on the daily routine. You have to challenge yourself to work on your plan to turn your dreams into reality.

Always remember, "You are not alone in this world. You have your dreams to conquer."

"A dream does not become reality through magic; it takes sweat, determination, and hard work."

- Colin Powell

CHAPTER 2

CHASE THE LAZY GOOSE

Laziness occurs when you don't want to face challenges. Most of the time it happens when we don't seem to care mentally and physically. In other words, lazy people do not possess the strong desire to achieve great things in life. One of the biggest reasons is that they often have an unproductive to-do list or no list at all.

To tell the truth, I felt lazy to start this chapter. I thought "What is there to tell about laziness?" I have never overcome this virtue but I am trying my best to overcome it. As planned earlier, I started to work on my goals to finish the chapter today. Hope this chapter will be a personal reflection for those who wish to chase away their laziness and be highly productive.

Procrastination

Laziness is another form of procrastination. First laziness starts from the time we try to get up from bed by snoozing the alarm several times. Sometimes, I keep multiple alarms to avoid snoozing. Slowly, I tried many tricks one by one. I tried keeping my mobile or alarm a little far away from my bed so that I could force myself to get up from bed. Instead of a tone, I kept one of my favorite songs as an alarm. I even asked one of my close friends who is an early riser to call me for a week as soon as he woke up. Some tricks worked out well and today I am able to get up early on my own as soon as my alarm beeps. It is never an easy task to give up a habit immediately but it is worth giving up when you have a dream and a strong plan for success.

If you are an early riser, then prepare your own tea/coffee for the day. Sometimes being in your comfort zone is also laziness. Just step out from your circle and try making a difference. You will feel more brisk than you ever felt. Try to prepare coffee and share it with your loved ones that will create a magic in your life.

Exercise

Exercising is the easiest and best practice to overcome laziness. You can start right away with push-ups or sit-ups or else with short brisk walking, jogging or running. Keep it as a regular habit to overcome laziness. Physical activities will not only make us healthy but also make us feel better. Healthy exercise secretes endocrines which helps to keep us active and energetic. It also improves our mood and reduces stress level which ultimately leads us to be focused and productive.

5 minute rule

Pick out a task which can be done within 5 minutes. For instance, cleaning up your dining table, bedroom or kitchen or putting your dresses for laundry. Cleaning the mirror, window glasses or any other similar tasks. Start doing something which you feel comfortable with. You will notice the transformation slowly.

Motivation

Researchers have suggested that laziness is caused due to lack of motivation but in reality it is the lack of passion. It's the hidden boundaries in your mind that makes you stay at one place without moving further. Your thinking and imagination has a great impact on your thoughts, habits and actions.

Take time to ponder your feelings so that you react actively. Your chances of winning increase each time when you participate in an activity. Your progress towards achieving your goals will improve the quality of your life. Self-motivation helps us or rather leads us to the path of success and happiness.

Self-Assessment

Self-Assessment is one of the ways to overcome the things which are holding you back. You should assess your level of fatigue, stagnation, inspiration, and general laziness. Detecting the issues and dealing with them is the only way to chase laziness. Once you find out the reason, you can deal with it vehemently. If you are tired, take some rest. Change your schedule accordingly.

If you're feeling uninspired, consider what might inspire you. Change your daily routine. Try to treat your senses with love, kindness, food, sights, and so on. This will help you to reduce much of the laziness and resistance.

Rest

Laziness occurs when you feel tired and lack energy. If you are really tired then you need to take care of your relaxing hours especially the sleeping hours. Resting doesn't mean sitting on your couch or sleeping on bed for a longer duration. Giving rest to your body and mind is essential to be productive. Enough rest gives you the strength and energy to be active. Keep yourself active by doing some meditation or simple exercises. Take a walk in nature to get some fresh air.

Chunking

Chunking is the method of dividing your day into small amounts of time for specific tasks. If you have a big task to complete, then break the task into several smaller tasks. Complete those tasks one by one in a series, which saves your time and energy. This method can be applied to any herculean task, goal or an aspiration which you wish to succeed.

Replacing Habits

You can overcome the habit of laziness through daily productive actions and activities. You have to substitute your lazy habits with highly productive habits.

Immediate Action

Taking immediate action needs courage and strength. Start doing the pending tasks immediately. When you begin with the unfinished work and complete the task, your confidence level boosts up. Once you start completing the tasks immediately, you will overcome the greatest hurdles in life.

We have seen different aspects of chasing laziness but there is a special character of being lazy. The uniqueness of it is that lazy people are the smartest people in the world. Lordi states that, "the lazy person often uses their intelligence to find a loophole or shortcut to get something done in half the time."

"Laziness due to tiredness is acceptable but being persistently lazy is detestable."

"Take time to deliberate, but when the time for action has arrived, stop thinking and go in."

- Napoleon Bonaparte

CHAPTER 3

CLOCK YOUR TIME

Time

Spending time judiciously is a key strategy in Planning and decision making. It is a wise idea to create a to-do list and not-to-do list. Productivity is measured on the job accomplished in a stipulated time. It also depends on how well you manage your time and work efficiently. Time management skills are essential for being highly productive.

A time record or journal is a must to gauge your level of productivity. This will give you a better understanding of the work that has to be done as well as assist you determine whether you have completed what you needed. You can analyze and find out the productive time of your day and make use of it. Schedule your time and prioritize your work based on the importance.

The following steps will guide you to manage your time and work effectively:

- Divide your time like sprints.

- Complete your task one by one.

- Motivate yourself to do the list.

- Work consistently and deliberately towards your goal.

For instance, if you are interested in your fitness. Exercise at least for one hour. Divide the time of exercising in four quarters. Do weightlifting for 15 min, jogging for 15 minutes, cycling or swimming for half an hour. You can change your patterns according to your limitations. At the end of the day, you will feel bliss for accomplishing something worthwhile and better than the previous day.

Managing your time

We all know that time is a winged chariot but I would rather say it is a winged bird. If you hold it loosely, it will fly away, and if you handle it skillfully and carefully, it will stay with you. If you grasp it tightly, it will die. If you start piling up work, you will have no time to complete. You will end up being stressed out and broken. You would have seen or heard about people losing their lives because of high pressure and stress. If you are careless of what you do and waste your time then you will be in a wretched state. So, manage your time with care so that you have time to do everything which you desire. Real enjoyment begins when you redeem your time wisely.

Audit your time by selecting two or three days in a week. Track your daily activities on hourly basis. Set a timer for every hour. When the alarm goes off, note down the activities done during the previous hour. Record the details and categorize the activities. Select your own tool: Use a blank page of paper, a daily planner, a digital calendar, or a to-do list app (For ex. Google Calendar, Apple Calendar, Fantastical, Woven).

Time management is a productivity technique for efficiently allocating your hours in a day towards your priorities in personal and professional life. We need to investigate how we spend our time to solve our time management problems. By finding wasted hours and funneling them into worthwhile endeavors, paves way to success. Ask the following questions before you clock your time:

How much time do I spend on my goals or passion?

What is my time category?

Am I spending enough time for professional development?

Am I spending enough time for personal and family life?

How much time do I spend on destructive activities? Social media? Video Games? TV? Social Communication? Other Distractions?

How many of my hours are dedicated to health and/or self-care?

Our perception of time makes every hour productive. Suppose a particular task takes less than 5 minutes to complete but you haven't done it at the right time, then you end up without doing the task. Later you will be thinking and asking yourself, why didn't I do that easy task? The answer is because of your own thinking and priority. Your priorities change from time to time and you lose track of even important things that need to be done.

If you really want to know your priorities, look at where you spend your time. These priorities apply to both work life and personal life. People who chronically procrastinate tend to have higher levels of stress, poor sleep patterns and bad prospects. On the other hand, people who manage their time effectively are prosperous and highly successful.

Managing your time needs to become your daily practice. It should not be just a list with a vague sense of your priorities. It should sound consistent or deliberate. Managing your time must be an ongoing process which you follow no matter what hinders. You need to keep focused on your priorities throughout your journey. I remember one of the great speakers motivating words in almost all his workshops where he asks his participants to chant the following mantra to overcome their hindrances. He used to say, "Hey folks, tell yourself strongly and loudly twice or thrice that no matter what I am going to do it." This mantra works wonders not only to his participants but I am sure, you too can use it to witness the miracles in your life.

Do Nothing

Although it seems to be easy, it is a difficult task to do nothing. Find a time to do nothing. Doing nothing except to relax and calm your mind. During this time take a deep breath, slowly inhale and exhale and mainly disconnect from distractions. Be out of reach from your electronic gadgets. Follow some relaxation techniques which make you feel better. By doing so, you will receive the energy to be highly productive.

Clocking your time

Clocking your time is a way of time management that helps you to divide your day into time slots. Each slot is assigned to accomplish a specific task, or group of small tasks. Stick on to those tasks until it is accomplished. You decide on the task based on priorities set for the day or week. By doing so, you will be able to complete each task with high focus.

When you're crafting your day or clocking your time, give time to a short break to relax and refresh. You can take few minutes to walk in the garden or sip a cup of coffee/tea or play with your kids and pets. Some tasks that will take only a few minutes. I believe that except death everything else can wait a minute or two. There is no harm in a short pause or delay while we are humans. We are not machines but are humans made of not only flesh and bone but also with passion and emotion. I feel pity on those who say we can't wait and there is no time. At last, they have no time to

27

breathe at all. We all know that wasting time is wasting the resources which you have; therefore, use your time wisely and judiciously.

Clock your time meticulously so that you can fill your minutes, hours, and days with meaningful work and memorable life moments. At least, you spend most of your time being productive. Consider the following chart while managing your time.

- ✓ Official time

- ✓ Break time

- ✓ Coffee/meal time

- ✓ Exercise time

- ✓ Sleep time

- ✓ Friend's time

- ✓ Family time

"Stress is largely self-inflicted, so the ability to manage stress more effectively comes from managing oneself."

- Michael Hetherington

CHAPTER 4

BEAT THE STRESS

Stress has a greater impact on your energy level and productivity. Stress may be short term or long term. Diagnosing the stress at the right time saves your life from tragedy. Before you beat the stress, you need to know for certain what kind of stress you experience. Sometimes, stress helps you to perform better when you are in need. For instance, imagine that you are going to give a presentation or a speech before a certain group of audience. Before the presentation or speech you may experience stress which is acute in nature. This type of stress vanishes away once you start delivering the speech. In reality, it helps you to perform better. If you know how to beat that stress then you hone the skill or the art of presentation or public speaking.

Let us begin with the classification of stress. It is broadly classified into two type's namely acute and chronic stress.

What is an Acute Stress?

It is a kind of short-term stress which you can feel when doing a new or exciting task. It can be something painful for a short period. For instance, a long wait in the queue, delay of uploading or downloading a file, slow processes, petty arguments with spouse or other person. These kinds of stress do not last long but for a shorter period.

What is Chronic Stress?

Chronic stress tends to last long. If unattended at the initial stage then it is difficult to manage later. You may have chronic stress if you have debts, physical or emotional loss, unhappy marriage life, or critical issues at the workplace. Pay close attention to what creates tension for you and take measures if you experience a lot of stress for a long time. Try to fix your source of stress. When you have chronic stress, your body stays alert, even though there is no danger. Nothing is too late when you really want to be productive in your current situation.

You may encounter health issues such as;

o   Heart disease

o   Obesity

o   High/low blood pressure

o   Acne, Pain on neck, shoulder, back, …

o   Disorders including anxiety and depression

o   Mensuration

o   Pregnancy, Fertility

o   Some of the common sources of stress are:

o   Work pressure

o   Death of dear ones

o   Getting laid off

o   Retirement

o   Financial crisis

o   Sickness

o   Family issues

o   Divorcing

Consult a therapist

When you have feelings of panic, such as dizziness, rapid breathing, or a racing heartbeat.

When you are unable to attend function at home or work at your job.

When you have fears that you cannot control.

When you are having memories of a traumatic event.

Treating yourself

You can do the following to treat yourself:

- Make sure you get enough sleep

- Eat healthy food

- Stay hydrated

- Ensure adequate exercise

- Take more time for relaxation and fun

- Talk about it with someone you trust

Proven methods include:

✓ Yoga

✓ Meditation

✓ Mindfulness

✓ Other relaxation exercises

Stress and Productivity

In order to be productive, stress is required in life, but when it gets excessive, it can be fatal. Everyone is prone to stress at some stage of our life at different levels and at different times. When stress takes over our mind, it is extremely difficult for us to focus on whatever we do. It also makes us continuously worry about things which may or may not happen. It also creates anxiety and fear leading to less productivity. For instance, setting deadlines to complete a task in a workplace is essential but unnecessary deadlines increase stress and anxiety.

How to beat the stress?

There are certain things which we can do to beat the stress. Communication is a key element to identify and resolve stress issues. Identify the source of your stress and communicate it to the right person. If it is not possible then communicate with those who could help you to resolve the problem. On the other hand, find what works for you and make time for it. Try to challenge yourself and think of all the possibilities to succeed.

Staying connected

Try to keep in touch with your loved ones, friends, and family. Use a video or phone call to speak with them. Video calls are superior to phone conversations because being able to see someone's face makes a significant impact. Connecting with people who can increase your self-assurance and faith in your ability to accomplish will undoubtedly assist you or someone else.

Chatting

Chat with different people about different aspects of life. Don't focus on stressful situations which disturbs you. Don't talk about diseases, tragic events or fights rather talk about those things which create positive vibes. Share words of wisdom and faith. Chat about the things which bring you joy, peace, hope and harmony.

Reach out

You are not the only person being stressed, worried and frustrated. Try to reach out to someone you haven't heard from for a short time. Talk and share your feelings to someone who will feel comfortable talking with you. When you feel depressed it affects your ability to work. If you feel too stressed and worried then it is wise to seek help from a therapist. But, there are also some basic things which you can do before it.

Take a break

Research has proved that People who take proper breaks in their work schedule are able to work without stress.

Change working style

Stress increases when you are confined indoors. It increases as days prolong with routine work. One of the best ways to overcome it is to change your working style.

Identify the source

It is important to know your stress triggers. Sometimes people get angry and stressed when they are hungry. While some get angry at silly things and later regret it. When people are lonely they tend to get more stressed and there are times when they are tired they get stressed and shout at others. Whatever be the reason, you have the solution with you. No one needs to tell you what you need other than yourself. If you're hungry, angry, lonely, tired then eat, calm, spend time with loved ones, or sleep. By doing so, you will feel better and rejuvenated to be highly productive.

Train your mind

Everything lies in your thinking. Whatever you think you operate, attract and react to your thoughts. If your thoughts are pure and positive then you draw everything positive and peaceful. Train your mind to beat the stress and rudder to a serene atmosphere to enjoy the benefits of life. The storm and the wind don't blow your way when you are keen to adapt and adjust your sail. The journey becomes smooth when you select the right path.

"Take control of your emotions before your emotions take control of you."

- Scott Dye

CHAPTER 5

DRIVE YOUR EMOTIONS

Social isolation has a greater impact on our thoughts, feelings and behavior. Emotions directly or indirectly affect decision making, interpersonal relationship, creativity and of course productivity. Researchers say, "Emotions reflect in our words, voice, body language, and through our actions". In order to be highly productive, we need to take time to reflect on our thoughts before acting or reacting through our emotions.

People often say to control our emotions. Our emotions vary from time to time. In different situations, we encounter different kinds of emotion. When someone says to control emotions they try to control us but not our emotions. They know well that we have the power to control our emotions. To put it in another way, emotions are like driving a car, we have full control. It is left to us on how well we drive the car. If we drive in a pleasant manner, our life runs in a smooth manner. If we drive rashly then we need to face the consequences. You can drive slow or fast depending on the rules of the road and fellow travelers. If you don't drive carefully, then you land up hurting yourself and others. Some learn the lessons in an easy way while others learn it in a hard way. Some way or the other it teaches us a valuable lesson.

Learn to drive your emotions in a pleasant manner. There is joy in riding. You never realize until you drive long. Our journey is long with crossroads. Be wise in driving with the right kind of people, attitude and emotion.

Each one of us drives through different mood swings in a day. In most cases, our actions depend on our emotions and feelings during the day. Positive emotions help us to achieve our daily goals. It strengthens our mind and body to attract and accomplish good things while negative emotions work the opposite. Positive emotions increase productivity. For instance, your short positive response to an email or a message can change the mindset of others. Trying to respond with care creates stronger relationships.

Before dealing with emotions, we need to know the different kinds of emotions that control us predominantly. Emotions are also like colors which create different shades when mixed at the right proportion. Our life is a portrayal of a colorful tapestry of emotions. What are these emotions? Do they control us or do we control them? Why do we make such a mess in life with these

41

emotions? How do people control these emotions? Oh, I don't know how I feel now? My emotions go wild whenever I hear people say that you are an emotional idiot. But, deep down my heart I know that emotions carry values and help us to lead a better life.

Emotional awareness helps us to deal with any kind of situation. When we carry positive emotions we create positive vibes which in turn increases productivity.

Basic emotions are happiness, sadness, love, joy, hope, faith, anger, fear, loneliness, melancholy, jealousy, envy, pride, shame, guilt, empathy, gratitude, inspiration, forgiveness, hatred, disgust, and surprise. Other emotions pop up now and then based on situations. The basic emotions play a vital role in leading a successful life. We are prone to fall prey to some of the negative emotions which in turn topples our life to misery. We need to learn to drive our emotions carefully to achieve success. Emotional awareness paves way to happiness and prosperity. Let's see some of the emotions which help us to lead better lives.

Happiness

One of the best emotions in life is Happiness. Happiness is a pleasant emotion. Smile is the sub product. When your heart feels satisfied and content then you will feel happy and cheerful. You will put on the real smile which is the best jewel in the whole world. A happy person never wants too much of anything. Many desire to be happy but only few remain happy in their life. Happy people are those who have learned the art of driving their emotions in a positive way. High productivity is possible when you and those are you are happy.

Sadness

Sadness occurs when we lose something desirable in life. When you are not able to achieve your desires, you feel sad. It is natural to feel sad when you lose someone but brooding over it for a long time sickens your body and mind. It will never allow you to progress in life. Sometimes, it halts and changes your direction towards an undesired path. Sadness is also a form of depression that cannot be taken lightly. Sadness weakens your thinking and allows your mind to wander rapidly. It affects your concentration, memory, and decision making. Excessive sadness leads to emptiness, lack of interest and motivation.

There are few ways to drive out sadness and depression. You need to engage yourself in activities that make you feel comfortable and interested. Start concentrating on your hobbies or play or spend time with little children. Listen to your favorite songs. When you are experiencing sadness or the worst situation, do not judge yourself or others. It will lead to more depression. If you want to cry then cry out loud and cry more till you have no more tears to shed. Take a short expedition. Cheer up and enjoy life. Taking care of our emotional well-being determines the quality of life and success.

Anger

Anger is the mother of all notorious things. Other emotions, such as irritation, anxiety, tension, and shame, might be hidden by anger in such a way that they can emerge when it is suppressed. Anger kills most of the productive time as well as affects your decisions. An emotion like anger gives birth to hatred, prejudice, resentment, and predicament. If you are nervous and angry about silly things then you may fail miserably in big things.

Anger can be brought to control through various ways. Nothing happens all of a sudden and everything cures with proper therapy. Anger gives signals and warning which helps you to take control of the situation. You need to take caution of the early warnings. Your innate feelings are exposed through your instant action. Try to channel your rage into physical activities like athletics, exercise, or any other game that requires physical activity. Control your immediate reactions to things which stir up your anger. Be careful with the anger which kindles hatred, deal with it immediately. It could be eradicated through acts of kindness. The greatest weapon to eradicate anger is to possess the spirit of forgiveness.

Fear

As the saying goes, "A Coward dies many times before his death". Fear makes you die every minute and second. Most people are obsessed with fear of failures, fear of loss, fear of rejections, fear of conflicts, fear of relationship failures, fear of debts, and so on. Fear creates cowardice and it destroys the happiness of living in the present. Sometimes fear helps you to perform well. By confronting fear, one can overcome it. There is no other way to escape fear than to recognize and challenge it. All fear is pushed out by perfect love and desire for the ultimate objective, which also helps you to become stronger.

Loneliness

Loneliness has been a source of inspiration for creation of books, music, movies, art works, and other creative skills. Loneliness gives you the freedom to explore and learn the values of life and survival. During the period of loneliness, we will have mixed emotions, thoughts and feelings which needs to be channelized to increase productivity. Loneliness can be for a shorter or longer duration based on situations and people. We must calmly watch, comprehend, realize, and learn the lessons that help us advance and evolve throughout those times.

Loneliness can also occur through abandonment. It may lead to depression and anxiety but we must realize that it is the time to strengthen your determination and lay a strong foundation. Sitting and brooding over the pain drowns you and your life. You need to overcome the situations and steer your ship to the destined path.

Loneliness is a feeling which sparkles in your thoughts that makes you feel lonely and isolated. There are people who feel happy being alone. They progress in their lives with a different set of thoughts and behavior. They try to make plans to deal with emotional and physical loneliness. Loneliness can be cured by making new connections, cultivating friendships, creating new habits, connecting with new people, places, and cultures.

Joy

Joy is evoked when you start enjoying the little things in life. A contented heart always makes you feel happy. People who are happy tend to be more joyful and they make people around them happy. A joyful heart is the best medicine in the whole world. Joy and Happiness elevates your immune system which results in productive work. Joy arises when you have a sense of satisfaction and contentment.

Whenever I think of the word "Joy", I always remember Richard Wagner quote, "The joy is not in things but in us". Definitely, your Happiness lies under your control. Turn towards the things which make you feel happy and joyful. When you start doing things which make you and people around you happy then it is a sign that you are leading a healthy, productive life.

Love

Love plays its foul play not only among youth but also among children and older generations. Excess love leads to possessiveness which turns out to be a torture to those who fail to reciprocate. Sometimes it's just the opposite where not an iota of love is received for those who wish to share their love. Genuine love is rare to be found at certain places. Fake love is in abundance to mar even the very life. We do find pure love such as mother's love, father's love, child's love, pet's love and so on. Each love acts as a zing to our life. No other emotion can teach and elevate us better than Love. Love the things which you do to increase productivity.

There are certain periods in our life when we feel lonely, deserted and empty and longing for love. Life gives chances to overcome so grab those opportunities without delay and press forward in these situations. Later, you will realize that these things don't matter in the long run. Always remember that true love makes your life colorful and meaningful.

Hope and Faith

Social isolation may occur due to loss of a family member, life partner, friends, or someone dear through death or confinement. It may also happen at old age when isolated from dear ones and society. During those periods, you may feel that it is hard to manage but you need to understand that you can overcome it through your strong will power. The power and faith within you helps you to stay strong. The hope which is in you will surely make you progress further in your life to achieve excellence. Hope gives the confidence to achieve our goals while faith does miracles in your life.

Gratitude

The law of Gratitude states, "If you are to get the results you seek, it is imperative that you should act on and obey this law." When you practice the law of gratitude in your life then everything falls into harmony. Your thoughts, feelings, attitude and actions reflect positive and productive vibes. Gratitude tends to work wonders in physical, mental and emotional well-being. Be grateful for everything in your life.

Miscellaneous

There are certain kinds of emotions which are dangerous. Emotions such as jealousy, hatred, envy and pride. These are never to be discussed or experimented. The very idea of thinking about the topics would weaken our body, mind and soul. It is better to be far from these emotions to save your life. Eradicate the very thought of it to lead a better, healthy and prosperous life.

The Crux of Driving your Emotions.

Stop worrying about the situation and don't think too much about what went wrong or whom to blame. Know the desires of your heart and cultivate joy, peace, love and gratitude. Don't ever complain and stop judging others as well as yourself. Be thankful in everything and in all circumstances. Spend time with those who respect your love. Cling on to the unconditional love of the Creator.

During the period of social isolation, there will be mood swings which either lifts you up or pulls you down. You need to handle these emotions and moods in a careful manner. Start your day with a prayer or meditation and proceed as per your plan. Don't ever give up your passion or goal for anything else. It may be a dull or energetic day based on how you start your day and lead the rest of the day.

It is important taking a few minutes to consider your current emotions rather than obsessing over the things that have been lost. By doing so, you will be able to come to a normal state after asking lots of questions to yourself and the situations. You will not be able to get answers to all our questions but you will be able to identify the worthiness of the situation.

Productivity depends on how we drive our emotions into a positive and healthy manner. To be mentally strong, you need to gain control over your emotions. Just like any other life skills, driving your emotions needs regular practice and determination.

"Successful people are simply those with successful habits."

- Brian Tracy

CHAPTER 6

REINFORCE HABITS

Habits cling on to us very firmly and determine our behavior most of the time. We can be productive or destructive based on our habits. Habits are a natural process and it takes time to cultivate or drop a habit. It is based on our interest, purpose and reward system. If you want to be highly productive, you need to reinforce habits that add value to your progress. Certain habits block the progress of your work and hinder your progress. It is hard to break those habits all of a sudden.

Certain habits block the progress of your work and hinder your progress. It is hard to break those habits all of a sudden. Reinforcing certain good habits through strategic processes changes our life for the better. Reinforcing habits comes out of a positive attitude to achieve the desired goals. If you are not able to achieve your goals hitherto, you need to consider making necessary changes to your daily activities and   reinforce your habits for positive results.

Build new habits into your schedule and follow them consistently. To ensure that you never give up, make a firm decision and fortify both your body and mind. Most productive people follow a few habits that are found common. If you are able to follow those habits and perfect them in your life, you will be highly productive. Here are some of the habits which are recommended by professionals and productive people around the world.

Productive Habits

Planning Activities

Plan your activities for each day and prioritize the activities to get down first. Prepare your mind to do major activities at the start of the day. It makes you feel more productive and will elevate you to accomplish more.

Staying on one task

Concentrate on fewer things and stop multitasking. Do one task at a time. Try to take one activity at a time so that you're completely focused on it. If you have many activities to do, select the top 5 and work on it. Forget about the rest of the activities while doing the top list. Later, you can follow the same thumb rule and complete the other tasks step by step.

Being Consistent

Consistency is the secret mantra for success. Being consistent should be your primary and ultimate goal. Being consistent should be a habit which will create a lasting impact.

"Look at a stonecutter hammering away at his rock, perhaps a hundred times without as much as a crack showing in it. Yet at the hundred-and-first blow it will split in two, and I know it was not the last blow that did it, but all that had gone before." – Jacob A. Riis

Avoiding distractors

Observe your daily activities and pick out the distractions. It may be social media, games, entertainment, chatting, or something else which obstructs you in achieving your goal. Try to eliminate those distractions by reinforcing new and healthy habits.

"Motivation is what gets you started. Habit is what keeps you going."

- Jim Ryin

Personal Habits

You need to give attention in developing your personal habits such as, grooming yourself, following a healthy diet, giving personal time for relaxing, developing new skills, learning and updating and honing your skills.

Boredom

After setting your goals and strategies, the foremost thing which disturbs your mind is boredom. You have to allow your mind to wander. It invents new things but sometimes it kills productivity. Boredom occurs due to lack of motivation and you need to take control over it. Boredom occurs when we have the feeling that the things which we do are not so important enough. This feeling brings down our morale and kills our creativity and productivity in a greater way. There are many ways in which you can overcome this boredom. You have to relax a little while, listen to music, read something interesting, take a walk or ride in your bike, or do some activities that stimulate energy which in turn results in productivity.

Engage Yourself

Join online communities according to your passion. Make new connections with people who can inspire you. You can also join groups involved in music, art, inspiring personalities, and so on. Engage yourself instead of being idle and whiling away the time.

Gaming

Gaming is fun which kills boredom at a great level but you should take care not to be addicted. Spend an hour or two on games which refreshes your mind and body.

Music

Music soothes the heart and mind. You can delve into the past, present and future with plenty of thoughts to inspire and motivate yourself. Make it a habit to listen to good music that changes your mind and lifts your soul to achieve something better.

Taking Risks

If you want to be highly productive, it is essential to take risks. Don't fear to try and fail. Failures teach lessons that will help us to grow. Successful people have failed many times in their life. Road to success is not a cake walk. You need do your best, challenging and progressing in spite of all barriers. You can achieve your goals by analyzing your risks and reinforcing specific habits that are productive. Take intelligent and calculated risks in a smart way to be highly productive.

Reward Yourself

There is no harm in celebrating your every little achievement. Give credit to yourself when you complete every small task. It boosts up your morale. If you can't give credit to yourself then who else on earth can do it. Give rewards to yourself.

Taking Breaks

Take short breaks to energize yourself and resume your work with a positive feeling. Taking short breaks helps you to get the required energy and strengthens physically and mentally to focus on future tasks.

Avoid multitasking

Multitasking doesn't keep the momentum, it hinders concentration and productivity. When you do multiple tasks at a time, you tend to fall short in completing the tasks. Highly productive people spend more hours on a single essential task to produce the best result. So, stop juggling multiple tasks and concentrate on one task at a time.

Saying 'Yes' and 'No'

People have a tendency to make more difficulties because they have a habit of saying "Yes" to a lot of things and "No" when they don't have to. Because they are used to say "Yes" and "Yes" all the time, and occasionally find it painful to say "No." These people constantly worry about what will happen, what the other person will think of them, whether they can handle the situation, and other similar questions. Most of your tension will go if you can learn to say "No."

Be bold to say 'No" at certain places where you have to say 'No". Saying 'No' does not mean that you can't do it, rather you are saying the fact that you prefer not to do it at that moment or point of time. If people cannot understand your 'No' then they will never understand you nor your work at any cost. If they understand you then they know that it is not the right time to ask.

Some years ago, I read an article on "How to say 'No' in 101 ways?" The information in the article was mind blowing and I learned to say 'No' in different ways which made me concentrate more on my goals. It changed my working style and many wondered whether I said Yes or No. Later they understood that it was a plain blunt 'No'. There were no hard feelings. After all, it made me more productive than before. Be wise in saying 'Yes' and 'No'.

Managing money

Managing money is a habit that helps you to lead a happy life. It is not essential to earn lot of money, but managing money should be a habit for a wealthy lifestyle.

Know your financial situation and plan your spending. Create a budget and strictly adhere to the budget. Being in debt is not a bad thing but piling it up is risky. Work out plans to eliminate debt and build savings so that you are far from a stressful life. Creating a multi-source of income will resolve most of the financial problems and create economic stability and freedom.

"Take care of your mind, your body will thank you. Take care of your body, your mind will thank you."

- Debbie Hampton

CHAPTER 7

BEING FIT

We all know that being fit and healthy involves activities that make different systems of our body in good condition. If you follow the right diet and practice the right activities, you will have the benefit of leading a healthy life. Be confident and say to yourself that I'm fit and healthy. When you are fit, you are far from illnesses such as BP, cholesterol, diabetes and so on. You can also feel young, energetic, and enthusiastic.

During isolation, we are prone to less movement and end up burning less calories. Researchers say that you have the risk of getting cardiovascular diseases when you sit more than 2 hours at one place. When we remain at the same place isolated and inactive, our metabolism tends to slow down. So, start doing some activities that boost your metabolism. Burning calories through workouts and games keeps your body and mind healthy. Maintain your body and give proper care and attention to your health until it is too late.

Living a healthy lifestyle is not necessary to be fit. We can stay fit by reducing our calorie consumption and exercising with body weight at a balance of high and low intensities. Additionally, staying fit increases our longevity and immunity.

Why is health and fitness required during social isolation?

Exercise and physical activities produce immediate and long term benefits. It reduces the risks of getting cardiovascular disease, diabetes, and other illnesses. It makes sure you are fit mentally and physically. It also improves the quality of your life.

What type of health and fitness do we need?

Keeping yourself fit can be of any sort. For instance, play your favorite sport, dance to your favorite music, or hit the gym. Always remember, if you are a newbie to lifting weights or a specific form of functional exercise make sure you seek professional help to start the journey. Make an effort to engage in some form of sweat-inducing exercise. Make sure you were active all day long to avoid being exhausted at night.

"Your body holds deep wisdom. Trust in it. Learn from it. Nourish it. Watch your life transform and be healthy."

What are the lifetime benefits?

You can increase your strength, flexibility, mobility, and endurance. You will be able to have a healthy life. It will make you feel lighter and younger even at old age. You will also have a healthy mindset. Ultimately, you can spend more quality time with your family and friends for a long time.

Why is health and fitness required during social isolation?

Fitness is not just for building muscles but it's all about having a healthy body. Isolation weakens our body and mind which results in poor health conditions. A healthy body creates a healthy and peaceful mind. When our body supports us, we can have a healthy life. Fitness is essential for each and every person.

What type of health and fitness do we need?

Fitness depends upon age and weight factor. For instance, when we are 60 or 70 years old, we do not care much about the shape of the body but we do care about how well we can move and it requires certain fitness activities to keep us energetic. We have to follow a lifestyle that keeps us healthy and fit. Whether you follow your own diet or the one prescribed by your dietician, you need to strictly follow the diet and fitness that is needed for your age and body.

Here are some useful tips to stay healthy:

- Don't sit in a place for more than 60 min. Try to move from your seat at regular intervals.
- Make sure you eat nutritiously and drink plenty of water.
- Eat lot of protein rich food
- Get a 7-8 hours of sleep
- Do lot of physical activity
- Lead stress free life
- Workout for minimum 30 to 40 minutes everyday

The benefits of FITNESS:

Reduces your body fat

Reduces your cholesterol and blood fats

Reduces blood pressure

Decreases your risk of heart disease

Decreases your risk of osteoporosis

Decrease your risk of arthritis

Increases your metabolic rate

Increase your endurance and flexibility

Enhances your sleep

Slows down the aging process

Boosts your mood and energy

Relieves stress and improves memory

Fitness is a way of life which leads to a healthy lifestyle. The common way to maintain a healthy life is to consume a healthy diet and follow regular exercise or physical activity. Fitness is stabilized by performing certain forms of activities that keeps you physically active. A sound synchronized physical and mental health is important at all times and especially during isolation. The body is a piece of machinery that has to be in constant motion along with other elements like sound sleep and a balanced diet. Fitness overpowers stress, regulates your mind and body. It releases positive hormones that give a structure and routine to a healthy and productive life.

Three Mantras of healthy lifestyle

Healthy lifestyle begins by giving an early start to the day with a good night's sleep.

Eating a healthy and balanced diet (carbs, fats, proteins and fiber) on time with adequate hydration.

Incorporating proper fitness regimes like brisk walking, yoga, cross fit, weight lifting, stretching, swimming and so on. Follow whatever suits your interest and consistency is the key.

"To ensure good health: eat lightly, breathe deeply, live moderately, cultivate cheerfulness, and maintain an interest in life." – William Londen

Your body is special. It is a product of billions of years of evolution and consists of trillions of cells that work together to produce a single, extremely complex, durable, and adaptable biological machine. Its level of health will dictate the quality and length of your life. Its level of fitness will dictate where you can go, what you can do, and how far you can get. Its appearance will dictate people's perceptions of you and the standard of the partners that you can attract. The good news is that all of these properties — health, fitness, and appearance — can be significantly improved with regular training.

"Rest and self-care are so important. When you take time to replenish your spirit, it allows you to serve others from the

CHAPTER 8

SELF-TIMING

Beginning the day of an especially challenging day, I felt disturbed to sit down on my sofa with coffee to drink, sipping my coffee and thinking deeply for a few minutes. Suddenly, I was clouded with thoughts and anxieties of the day which took me far and wide. Slowly, I put aside all my thoughts and planned to sit back and rest, I realized that my anxiety began to fade away by enjoying my cup of tea. Yes, it was my cup of tea which was specifically prepared by my spouse. It was not a regular coffee. Sometimes, we need to take time to enjoy the present.

There are times when we need to give attention to the details and changes that happen in our life. I would have missed the taste of tea while delving into my anxieties but luckily I was able to enjoy the moment. It was made possible because of giving time to enjoy the little things in life. In the fast moving world, we need to take time for self-care. When we are too busy, we forget to enjoy life. Little things in life create wonderful memories that should never be missed at any stage of our life. Try to get lost in finding yourself.

Allocate time to find yourself so that you can see the transformations that occur in your life. Although it seems so easy at the outer layer, the process of finding yourself is a difficult task. We all have the power to control stress but we lose control when it gets long and tough. We tend to get overstressed and fail to complete the tasks which lead to many other mishaps. If we analyze the situations, the evidence will be so clear that we require some time for self-care to strengthen us. It is the right time to think about personal productivity, and then get the other things done.

If you desire to be highly productive, you need to take time for yourself and your resources. If you have enough energy and strength to fight your battles, nothing hinders your way. You need to spend some time analyzing and knowing how to challenge your hurdles. Life's battles are won through resilience, affirmation, positive and strategic thinking.

You need to take a break and pull yourself to take care of your mental and physical health. When you feel hard and overwhelmed, it is necessary to take a break and contemplate on the work which you do. Pick out the things which are essential to your life and leave out the rest. Spend time with people who transform your life into a better personality. Sometimes it is better to be away from those things which affect your progress whether it's your job, friends, relatives or relationships. True happiness lies in what you do with your passion and independence. When you live your true self then you can lead a life full of happiness and prosperity.

Finding Yourself

The greatest adventures and truths of life lie in self-discovery. Knowing yourself and setting self-oriented goals empowers your life and boosts up your confidence and motivation. It also helps to recognize our potentials and be open to challenges that provide opportunities and experiences. Knowing what we want is fundamental to finding ourselves.

"Relax, Recharge, and Reflect. Sometimes it's OK to do nothing."

- Izey Victoria Odiase

Self-expression

In every walk of our life, we portray ourselves to others and leave a trace of ourselves. Expressing your true self in all circumstances is not possible but the power of self-expression lies in portraying our real and authentic self. Any false expression of your real self can lead to adverse effects. If you are not able to express yourself, you may end up in a different path which is not meant for you. Sometimes you will regret a lot for losing the great opportunity. Whatever be the situation, make use of the situation to represent and express yourself.

Creativity

Creativity sparks when you delve deep into your mind. You come out discovering novel ideas. Spending time for yourself enhances divergent thinking and boosts creativity. It creates opportunities to express whatever you feel and want. It paves way for us to share hidden thoughts and creative works such as paintings, drawings, writing, and performing arts evolve in the process. All creative works flaunt our own uniqueness and acknowledge us. It also involves our willingness to open your mind, heart and soul.

Creativity stirs up self-expression which is an expression of your emotions, thoughts and beliefs. When you start exploring your mind, you tend to discover yourself. Ultimately, it improves your mental health and well-being.

Happiness

Understanding the meaning and purpose of life is vital to discover who you are and what makes you happy. It is a known truth that happiness lies with our perceptions and mostly within ourselves. Happy people create a positive vibe around themselves and others. They are more successful in personal and professional life.

Happiness helps us to be highly productive and successful. Learn to be happy with yourself first and then everything around you turns out to be pleasant and amazing. Do things which make you feel happy. Whether it's playing with your pet, painting a canvas, decorating your home, cooking your favorite meal, renovating your garden or anything which makes you feel content and satisfied.

The reason why happiness is of prime importance is that it gives us the power to achieve our goals and ambitions in life. Being happy will not only make us a pleasant person but it has the potential to change the lives of others. The cup of joy overflows around you and on those who genuinely love and care for you. They will see and feel the difference in you and in their lives.

Perception

We live in an ever changing and constantly progressing fast-paced society, which makes it difficult to craft our time to be in our real self. Our views and works depend on others' expectations. You tend to lose everything and also yourself in this scenario. It is not wise to lose yourself in pursuit of something that the world requires. Disconnecting ourselves from the present lifestyle for a little while allows us to reconnect ourselves with the way we perceive the world. It allows us to improve our perceptions.

You are better able to empathize and communicate with others when you are aware of who you are and what you are capable of. In an effort to find yourself, you must first know your life's purpose. Here are some of the questions which will guide you to have a varied perception:

What do you need in life?

What does the world want from you?

What is your passion?

What is your mission?

What are your strengths?

There is no right or wrong way to find your personal sense of purpose but it is essential to ask yourself and find out the meaning of your life. Psychologists say that our perceptions are our reality. It molds and shapes our experiences. It also keeps us focused and clear on what really matters to us and what we want in our life.

You don't require an accurate perception of your reality but you need to take enough time to discover the reality which you are going to create. It simply means asking yourself what your values are, what really matters to you, and then later pursuing those principles which you believe.

Focus

Spending quality time being alone will allow you to be more focused on your goals. It also gets rid of unnecessary thoughts that hinder your progress. It allows you to refocus on your own priorities and work out plans to achieve in your life.

The major benefits of spending quality time for yourself are:

- Increases Productivity

- Reduces Stress

- Improves Relationship

- Recognizes Personal Strengths

- Boosts memory and creativity

- Develops Empathy

- Identifies Priorities and opportunities

- Strengthens emotions and Builds confidence

Sometimes you need to help yourself so that you don't need to depend on others all the time. We need to spend time being alone to reflect and progress. Who knows the real potential within you? It is you and you alone who can bring out the hidden power. Spend more time with yourself and being yourself to enjoy the boons of life.

"It is impossible to produce superior performance unless you do something different."

- John Templeton

CHAPTER 9

CREATIVITY

Thinking out of the box while dwelling inside the structured box never helps you to be productive. Thinking out of the box is critical in today's innovative driven businesses and economy. Many entrepreneurs and business ventures rely on creative ideas and methods to be successful. As an individual or entrepreneur, the ability to come up with innovative ideas by thinking out of the box is a valuable asset.

Thinking outside the box is an inborn quality, it is a skill that needs to be honed. The more you sharpen it, the better you will excel in it. One of the methods to think outside the box is by changing your perspective of looking into a situation. Allow your brain to contemplate divergently regarding the regular situations. By doing so, you will allow your mind to rigorous and lateral thinking to resolve an issue. When you start thinking outside the box, you realize that there are lots of solutions and opportunities to deal with the problems which you face in life.

The present world is obsessed with time and productivity. People are hired to be highly productive. Companies train people to accomplish their tasks in a systematic way. They want their employees to be less creative and highly productive. Most people often think that creativity has nothing to do with productivity because it is just the opposite. They also think that creativity takes time to grow and flourish. But, we need to understand that creativity and productivity are intertwined and they work together to sustain productivity.

Highly productive people are those who come up with innovative ideas and solutions for efficiency and progression. Depending on individual, profession, and business motives creativity and productivity play its role at different proportions. When productivity comes to a halt creativity gives hand to resume and progress. In the same way, all creative ideas are made null and void if not converted into reality.

Thinking out of box is all about exploring innovative ways to face issues, challenges and complicated situations. Some of the ways to improve creative skills are as followed:

- ✓ Learn new skills

- ✓ Know different cultures

- ✓ Learn different language

- ✓ Religion

- ✓ Read a novel

- ✓ Watch different genres of movie

- ✓ Try poetry or short story

- ✓ Draw or paint a picture

- ✓ Play a new game

- ✓ Do a performance like singing dancing or miming

- ✓ Push your boundaries

Creative ideas need to be transformed to productivity. When creativity and productivity go hand in hand, we tend to approach problems in a different perspective, and understand the situations in a better way than we thought earlier. Perhaps one of the most effective methods to be highly productive is to hone the creative skills.

Seven Mantras to boost Creativity and Productivity

- Creativity is ignited through new explorations and experiences while productivity is attained through efficiency and consistency.
- Take regular breaks from your routine to increase productivity. Try to switch off from your regular work and give room to creativity.
- Brainstorm your ideas to unlock creativity and build on to increase productivity.
- Learn new skills that help to improve creative thinking and upgrade with emerging technologies to increase productivity.
- Think out of box to resolve problems in a different perspective and mitigate risks to improve productivity.
- Manage and give time and space to nurture creativity and productivity.

"Sometimes the most productive thing you can do is relax."

- Mark Black

CHAPTER 10

3R'S

Everything in this world happens according to its time. There is a time to be born and a time to die. A time to create and a time to destroy. A time to refrain from anger and a time to get anger. A time to hold your peace and a time to lose it. Each and every event occurs at a particular time. Likewise, before any productivity there is a time of incubation which requires utmost attention.

The time of incubation is a mystery even to the greatest researchers. Let us consider our life in relation to the process of incubating chicken eggs or the metamorphosis of butterflies. There are some stages in our life where we are subject to the process of incubation. Only few people are aware of it but most of them don't realize or understand the process. They try to come out of their shell and suffer greatly. They become incomplete and feel void in their life. Those who anticipate the change hold their patience and survive the process. They stay at rest to adapt to the situations and embrace the changes in the journey of metamorphosis. Those who survive this process flap their wings with flying colors.

People who are successful in their life follow the principle of Rest, Renew, and Rejuvenate (3Rs) during the incubation period to be highly productive. The first step is staying at rest in the process of incubation. It is essential to rest but not too long. You need to take rest for a while and then keep moving, adapting to the changes. Proper rest to mind and body promotes mental health, releases stress, and boosts immunity, creativity and productivity.

Rest is often connected to physical tiredness which requires body rest like sleep. If you are deprived of sleep, you tend to feel tired. The loss of sleep leads to drowsiness, stress, lack of focus, blood pressure and other health issues related to the cardiovascular system. Rest is not only related to physical but also mental and emotional. When you are overloaded with the day's work, you feel exhausted, tired and weak. Your body and mind needs rest to renew and resume to be productive. In addition, emotional rest is also essential to face the challenges of personal and professional life. If you wish to be highly productive in life, you need to pay more attention to your physical, mental and emotional well-being.

Rest can be any form of activity which restores energy and provides relief from pain and stress. There are various ways by which you can practice taking rest. The methods vary from individual to individual. You can adopt any method that best fits you. Here are some of the proven basic techniques that can be useful:

- Do some breathing exercises for 3 to 5 minutes.
- Try stretching your body with light warm up activities.
- Take a short nap for 5 to 10 minutes.
- Spend time with nature.
- Spend time with kids or pets
- Listen to your favorite playlist
- Do massage or spa
- Take a shower or warm bath

The second step of incubation is to Renew. Renewing means reviving, re-establishing, replacing, extending and resuming. Reviving helps to feel fresh and regain strength. Re-establishing strengthens the bond, replacing clears the broken and worn out things, extending proves your validity, and resuming helps to begin again after interruptions. The process of renewing takes place within ourselves. Every single thing which happens in our mind is reflected through our body and actions. The mind and the thoughts decide our actions. Our thoughts create a great impact on our emotions and influence our actions. Renewing gives us new strength and life. It changes the quality of life and helps us to approach problems with different and new perspectives. When our mind changes everything around us changes.

Every one of us gets stuck in life at some point of life. We may feel that nothing works out as planned. We sometimes forget our real pursuit and get washed by the tides of life. At this juncture, renewing your mind, body and soul helps you to reignite and rediscover your dreams and passions. Self-renewal helps you to resume your journey with great strength and spirit. You cannot be productive unless you renew your mind. You need to fill your mind with positive and productive thoughts to be highly productive in your life.

Renewing gives you new strength to pursue your dreams and aspirations in life. It is one of the greatest tools which will keep you pressing forward with high productivity. Lay aside the old, unwanted and worn out things in your life that hinders your progress. Put away the thoughts and actions that pull down the productivity. Cultivate habits and actions that help you to reach the desired heights.

"The time to relax is when you don't have time for it."

- Sydney J. Harris

The process of renewal happens when you start finding yourself. Sometimes you need to take the journey towards spiritual renewal to accomplish your mission. There are various ways to explore and experience self-renewal. You can devise your own method of renewal or follow some of the following ways to renew yourself.

- Offer your assistance to those in need. Social and emotional well-being are developed through this act of service. You might also sign up with a nonprofit organization.

- Be one with nature. Dive into a river, do gardening, soak in music, explore through hiking or trekking.

- Take a short or long distance ride.

- Take a day off from electronic gadgets and spend time with people, pets, indoor and outdoor activities.

- Take a visit to an orphanage or elderly home.

- Spend time in holy places, scriptures and divine activities.

- Spend quality time with quality people.

The final step is to rejuvenate. This process makes you feel young and energetic. There are no hard and fast rules or methods. It varies from person to person. You need to pick out techniques that rejuvenate yourself.

There are few easy methods that can be implemented in your daily life to make you feel rejuvenated. As said earlier, the first step is to reduce your screen time on mobile phones, television or computers. The next step is to take a few minutes' walk to breathe fresh air. Spend time in nature like gardening, bird watching, and so on. Involve in some outdoor activities or community services. Keep yourself active and energetic. Follow activities that make you feel young and energetic. Spare time to adorn yourself with outer and inner beauty.

Make necessary changes to maintain the health of your body, soul and mind. Then, you'll find yourself feeling more focused and level-headed — and happy. You'll feel content knowing that your preparation efforts were successful once you start accomplishing more. Overall, your productivity will reflect in more areas in your life than just one, giving you more time to spend on what truly matters.

"When you take time to renew, restore, and rejuvenate yourself, you send a message to your body, mind, spirit and whole being that you are worthy and deserving of all the good they have to offer. And in return, they will shower you with clarity, inner peace, good health, love, and serenity."

- Luminita D. Saviuc

SUMMARY

Productivity should be an essential focal point for anyone who wants to live a more fulfilling life. Be thankful for everything in life. Give thanks for all the good and bad things in life as it teaches you to progress. Productivity isn't just about getting work done; it's about using your time effectively to live the balanced, fulfilling life you want to live. Feeling satisfied and fulfilled about what you are doing is the essence of great productivity.

The following points are worthwhile to consider for productive life:

Find which productivity method works for you, and start sowing and reaping the benefits.

- Craft your day depending on your priorities.

- Motivate yourself to take immediate actions on pending

 tasks.

- Clock your time judiciously.

- Train your mind to beat the stress.

- Drive your emotions into a positive and healthy way.

- Build healthy habits that helps you to progress personally and professionally.

- Follow regular routines to keep yourself fit and healthy.

- Spend quality time to take care of yourself.

- Develop creative skills.

- Take time to renew, restore, and rejuvenate yourself.

"Enjoy the little things in life and bigger things will be on the way."

Raja Mathangi (Santhose Kumar) linked through my connections was an engineering graduate in India when we lastly met in person. He had pursued his passion and has become an Advocate in Madras High Court in the recent past. When I looked into his profile, I discovered that he is running a charity for education to people from all strata of the society by providing concessions, scholarships and assistance to children from poor, needy and deserving families. The trust was under the name of **Mathangi Charitable Trust** which was established on 8th of April 2015.

The **main objectives** of the trust are: establishing educational institutions, providing equal opportunities for education by linking children from poor families with sponsoring families /individuals/corporate, evolving systems of educational outreach programme, conducting vocational training centers, undertaking humanitarian social works, and also providing shelter and care for the mentally challenged particularly those suffering from schizophrenia and allied illnesses.

He wrote in one of his mails that poor people and servants of god were starving for food and basic amenities during quarantine period. There were around 1500 families in Chennai and around the city under his surveillance who were at the verge of ending their life due to lack of support and guidance.

He received donations and charity from colleagues and friends which was only sufficient to save few families. His passion and prayers to help the needy burns deep within him and the volunteers of Mathangi Charitable Trust. Personally, I was interested in the objectives of the trust where they wished to contribute to the welfare and amelioration of the poor, orphans, windows, destitute, physically handicapped, socially and economically weaker sections of the people and so on. The charity solely spends the money for the welfare of the humanity.

I have decided to donate 10% of my profits to the Charity. Including the sales of my books, workshops and seminars. If you wish to make donations, just contact the Managing Trustee "Mathangi Charitable Trust" or through social media platforms.

Helping Hands

www.ingramcontent.com/pod-product-compliance
Lightning Source LLC
Chambersburg PA
CBHW062333290526
45794CB00005B/2019

*   9   7   9   8   8   5   6   3   9   9   7   1   3   *